The Essence of Water

Oceans Earth and Us

Healing Our Relationship with Water

& Save Our Oceans from Ocean

Acidification

Zoe Hudson

This book is dedicated to my Daughters and Grandchildren with love who all love the Sea, the Ocean and this beautiful Blue Jewel Earth.

The Invitation

I invite you to explore the element of water

within yourself, what that means to you and

in relation to others, in the light of truth that

all water is connected within ourselves, each

other and within this world you are a part of

For we are not separate, we are one.

The Essence of Water

Oceans Earth and Us

Remembering our deeper relationship with Water

and save our Oceans from Ocean Acidification.

The Essence of Water is a remembering of our deeper

relationship with the essence of water within ourselves, and

with the waters of the Earth. An opportunity to dive in to

inspiring information, creative story, poetry, and ecological

tips. All in relation to how taking care of the spiritual and

physical aspects of our whole selves, in relationship to the

Water, Seas and Oceans of our beautiful Blue Jewel Earth.

Which is of huge importance for maintaining a healthy

balance within us all and within the waters of this blue jewel

Earth now and for the future.

The Essence of Water – Healing Our Relationship with Water – Oceans Earth and Us environmental art exhibition has been exhibiting since 2012 in a variety of places in Devon and Cornwall UK

This year 2024 in my commitment to reach more people I decided to create this book which has been created with the resources that I have been sharing at my environmental art exhibition which I am now sharing with you, where I hope it can reach all those who are looking for a book just like this one.

Appreciations

Deep appreciation and love for the water, for the healing essence of water, within ourselves, the water, the rivers, the seas, the Oceans and the global Ocean, that exist with this beautiful blue jewel Earth we all call home. Also for my beautiful Daughters and for my Grandchildren whose love and presence inspires me to develop creative environmental projects like this small book. Created to inspire others in creating small changes internally and externally, which as we all know in time, eventually can grow in to expansive changes for the better. My husband too for his love and support with the preparation to publish this book. My dear parents for my first visit to the Atlantic

Ocean and for all the memorable times there.

My dear friends and teachers.-

Sue -Claire Morris, whose teaching inspired me to explore deeply with the natural environment and express creatively with story and movement.

Nancy Sherwood – Shamanic teacher, founder of Travellersjoy.ca who 1 have had the honour to know alongside Sue- Claire, experiencing the awareness of our oneness, exploring our sense of belonging on the planet and support from Nancy in creatively expressing this awareness through poetry, healing, art, dance and movement.

Lyn Whiteman- Art tutor and Neutral Space Relaxation founder, whose art tuition and relaxation sessions led to the creation of the painting – The Blue Jewel- for the Essence of Water Exhibition. Love &

appreciation for my family, friends, & for all life.

Contents

The Essence of Water

Introduction

Throughout my life my much loved holidays by the sea and by the Atlantic ocean in the UK have always instilled me with a sense of peace and a deep feeling of well being to me.

Later on in my life, I knew deep within that I needed to move myself and family closer to the sea for solace, peace and space. Many happy memories have been made by the sea and by the ocean which still continue to be made with my Daughters and our family.

Alongside living near the healing benefits of sea, such as the salty air, the salty water, the sound of the waves, the crystal clear water and expansive sea and horizon, all which support me with a feeling of being held, and rejuvenated. I began to also explore holistic well being therapies to support myself, I found these experiences to be beneficial and over the years I have studied a variety of courses and qualified in various well being modalities to support looking after myself and to share with others. The awareness of how important it is to tend to the well being balance within is a priority. I feel from being close to the sea, and immersing oneself in nature is truly restorative. I began to recognise how allowing time and space of tending to ones inner balance with nature was becoming profound. My love and appreciation for nature, especially for the sea was growing.

So in 2006 I started a Foundation Degree course in Environmental Art and rural crafts with Plymouth University, UK. I was very fortunate as the course was based at Bicton College, set within an area of outstanding natural beauty in Devon, minutes from the coast. During the Expressive art modules with teacher Sue – Claire Morris I was invited to explore my relationship with the earth and express this through poetry and storytelling. This was where my poetry and stories started. Alongside meeting Nancy Sherwood- Contemporary Shamanic teacher and friend, who guides people in to a deeper communion and commitment to the Earth, It was during my experiences with Nancy and Sue -Claire that the creative flow began to deepen with writing poetry, leading me to the creation of poetry and my book of poetry called I Mother Earth being written.

At a similar time I was receiving art tuition with Lyn Whiteman, a friend, artist tutor and well being practitioner. It was from an art and well being session with Lyn that then inspired me to paint the painting – Blue Jewel , which is my central artwork of The Essence of Water art and information exhibition.

I choose to write this book at a point in my life in the light of the enquiry in to the deeper meaning of relationship with myself, my family, the Earth and Oceans. This enquiry was and is alongside the light on the huge environmental issues such as Ocean Stressors, particularly Ocean Acidification which is accelerating at a rapid rate with alarming forecasts, if we continue as we are.

I believe we can all can connect with hope for the changes we wish for in the world. With my interest in the inter-connectivity of personal well being and how that relates to the well being of the Earth and global Ocean this deep interest ignited a sense of exploring how to support a healthy balance of health within the self and within the water, and within the Seas, Oceans and with the Earth.

It stirred a commitment within me to see what I could learn about these inter connected relationships and what can I as an artist and poet creatively express about it. Being one person yet knowing I am a part of a collective wave of many people who are making changes for healthier ways forward in ourselves, our families, our communities, together as humanity in harmonious relationship with each other, the Ocean and Earth.

Making conscious healthier choices for the well being of ourselves, for the Oceans and the Earth, which we are all urgently called to make, could ensure a more balanced level of health within ourselves, each other, the global Ocean and the Earth. How are we choosing to be with this Planet and Oceans and what legacy are we creating for the next generation? We can all make a difference by listening to the intuitive guidance within our own hearts, where we can be informed to awaken to the innate wisdom within each of us and realign with a more conscious way to live.

A way that naturally inspires us all to become more loving, harmonious, well and sustainable with our selves, each other, and with the Oceans and the Earth.

During a time of home educating my youngest Daughter, alongside studying as an Environmental Artist, I felt a deep interest to look at what would it take to support my Daughter for her to learn in a more holistic way in relationship to each other and the Earth.

I invited my Daughter to choose an interesting topic of choice from a variety that we spoke about that could encompass academic, artistic and experiential aspects of learning, together with an aim to be and learn outside as much as possible. Children's natural interests can be clear indicators as to what skills they have, to explore, develop and fulfil in their lives. My Daughter replied that she would like to learn about the seas and Oceans. Together we began on a deeply moving and meaningful chapter of our lives, exploring and experiencing at that time our local sea and coastline of Lyme Regis, Dorset in the UK. We made being and learning by the sea a daily event and together we began to discover things like – How connected we all are to water and that the Ocean produces at least 50% of the oxygen on Earth.

The Oceans produces the oxygen through the plants such as phytoplankton, kelp and algae plankton. Together we began to discover about our deeper relationship with the water and that we are the same ratio of water as the earth.

This experience alongside my studies in environmental art became the early foundation of the creation of The Essence of Water – Healing Our Relationship with Water and Save Our Oceans from Ocean Acidification environmental art exhibition and small book. This book has been created with the resources that I have been sharing at my environmental art exhibition which I am now sharing with you. The exhibition has existed since 2012, and I have exhibited it in a variety of places in Devon and Cornwall and recently felt it would be helpful to spread the awareness from the exhibition through the creation of a book, where I hope it can reach all those who are looking for a book just like this one.

The Essence of Water can inspire people through the marriage of environmental information and creativity which together can bring a whole awareness within, a balancing of the left and right hemispheres of the brain, left brain is more verbal, analytical and orderly, the right brain is more visual, intuitive and creative. Experiencing information and creativity together can potentially reach a deeper place within on how to re balance our relationship with the element of Water within ourselves, each other and with the Oceans of the Earth, which is the largest ecosystem of our planet. Becoming more aware of our deeper relationship with water, we can begin to awaken to the reality that healthy water inside of ourselves and within the Oceans of the Earth is vital in supporting life. Deeper insights into our relationship with the element of water, Oceans and Seas, can also assist us in to a deeper relationship with water. Alongside the understanding of how to become aware of making realistic everyday changes in reducing personal Co2 emissions, which together can all add up to a collective change consciously and environmentally. It is possible to shift in to more hopeful ways that can support a healthier balance of all life. As we remember what we love, we naturally protect what we love and we can all play a part in relation to consciously making a deeper re connective relationship with self, with each other, in relation to the whole global ocean and this magnificent blue jewel earth.

Chapter 1

The Essence of Water

Oceans Earth and Us

Every drop of water is a microcosm of the Universe

Quote from Ralph Waldo Emerson

The Essence of Water

Oceans Earth and Us

Healing our Relationship with Water

and Save Our Oceans from Ocean Acidification.

The Essence, meaning the intrinsic nature of something. In this case of Water, which is a deep discovery of how we can heal our relationship with the water within ourselves, and with the waters of the Earth. An opportunity to dive in to inspiring information, creative story, poetry and ecological tips that invites us in to the depths of exploring how to take more care of the spiritual and physical aspects of our whole selves. All in relation to taking better care of the water, the Oceans and of our beautiful Blue Jewel Earth, is of huge benefit for us all.

We are sensitive beings all related to water and to all the frequencies that water is exposed to, the water within our bodies and of the body of the earth is urgently calling for us to re-balance our relationship with the essence of Water, which is the essence of all life "we are all connected through the element of Water.

Our bodies have the same ratio of Water as the Earth, we could be seen as a micro of the macro, a mirror of the inner and outer. How-ever you choose to look at this, one can in their own way intuitively remember how we are all in relationship, with self, each other and the Earth, as a part of one whole living Planet. We are mostly water, approximately 70 %, and approximately the same ratio applies to the Earth. We receive approximately 50 % of our Oxygen from the Oceans. The Oceans produce the oxygen through plants such as phytoplankton, kelp and algae.

Water is the essence of all circulatory systems within our body and the circulatory system within the Earth, which is filled with the same rhythms and patterns. This also applies to the water element of the human body, the circulation of blood, and the heartbeat.

If these rhythms, experience anything that interferes with the process of life, such as interference's from the small subtle ill effects, such as negative thought patterns, behaviours and to microwave, electromagnetic stress, electromagnetic frequencies and the larger environmental issues, which all can contribute to human and environmental health issues. Over exposure to electromagnetic frequencies can affect the autonomic nervous system, which can alter the information that a body needs to maintain its life-force.

Electromagnetic frequencies can be harmful to our bodies and to all the living kingdoms of this Earth.

Modern lifestyles consisting of being indoors for long periods often disconnects us from nature, particularly of the water in the air, rivers, seas, and from the elements, which includes the earth.

In modern life, at home, work or school we are exposed to all kinds of microwave and electromagnetic stresses, mostly on a subtle level that can affect the molecular structure of the water within our bodies and that of the water within our rivers, seas and oceans. This can potentially contribute to human and environmental dis-ease, which could be preventable by adapting to more natural ways of living, working and learning.

Becoming more conscious of our deeper relationship with water, we can begin to acknowledge that healthy water inside of our- selves and within the Earth is vital, for water supports health and vitality for all life. We are all connected through the element of water, and we are collectively called to engage and deepen our relationship with the waters within ourselves and with the waters of the Earth. We are called to remember more of the whole picture of how important it is to love, respect and take care of the deeper reality of our watery body and the waters of the Earth. In this remembering, we can all begin to explore and make conscious changes for the future. Changes which can support the potential for a more harmonious, healthier, sustainable way forward for the health and future of ourselves, Humanity, the Oceans and for the Earth as one whole ecosystem. For our own health and for the health of the Planet, remembering to love, honour and nurture our true relationship with water is essential, for through water, the essence of all life, all is connected.

Presently the global Ocean is under stress from multiple stresses, which is having a tremendous impact on local, regional and global scales. One of the core issues that is stressing our global Ocean is the emissions that are created individually, collectively and globally, throughout our daily lives and activities.

Ocean Acidification (OA) is a term used to describe significant changes to the chemistry of the ocean-

Ocean Acidification occurs when carbon dioxide gas (or CO_2) is absorbed by the ocean and rapidly goes through a series of chemical reactions which increase the acidity of the surface seawater (lowering its pH) The Ocean has already removed approximately about 30% of anthropogenic CO_2 from the atmosphere over the last 250 years, which has caused a decreasing pH level, at a rate not seen for around 60 million years. This is happening at a speed 100 times greater than has ever been observed during the geological past. This effect has slowed the accumulation of CO2 in the atmosphere and the rate of global warming; without the ocean becoming a sink, atmospheric CO2 levels would already be greater. The Continuance of a rapid change to ocean chemistry is expected to be bad news for life in the sea. As well as causing problems for many organisms with calcium carbonate skeletons or shells such as oysters, mussels, corals and some plank tonic species. It could also impact many other organisms, ecosystems and processes with potential serious implications for society.

Acidity on average, of the upper ocean has already declined by around 0.1 pH unit (30% increase in acidity) since the industrial revolution and it is forecast to further decline by about 0.3 pH units by the end of this century if CO2 emissions continue at the present rate. Ocean Acidification can and is causing ecosystems and marine diversity to dramatically change. The impact could be substantial, on many levels and could have rippling consequences throughout the entire Oceanic ecosystem.

One of the most devastating impacts of rising ocean acidity could be the collapse of food webs. As ocean chemistry continues to change, the many goods and services they provide could dwindle, forcing millions of people to find new food sources, new homes and new sources of income. Adapting to these losses would take huge resources from the global community and in some cases adaptation would not be possible and the future of our Oceans is uncertain.

The Co2 emissions that are created from a highly industrial way of modern living, from our travel, our purchases, the use of energy in our homes are all part of our individual and collective additional Co2 emissions. Which is contributing to the strain on the sensitive ecological system of the Oceans and atmosphere. Recognising that everything we do effects our selves, each other, the Oceans, and the Earth, can empower change for the better.

To see clearly the whole picture of how crucial it is to respect and take care of the deeper reality of our watery body and of the waters of the Earth, we can then begin to make very conscious changes for the better, now and for the future. Changes which support a more harmonious, healthier sustainable way forward for the health and future of humanity, the Oceans and for the Earth. A more promising future is one where we reduce carbon dioxide emissions, transition to cleaner, renewable sources of energy and prevent the need for such large-scale adaptation. Commitment is being called for, to love, respect and nurture the waters within our bodies, and the waters of the global

Ocean. In acknowledgment of the deeper truth of the part we all play in the well-being of our own personal health and the health of the Waters of the Earth, which has become an urgent call for change. Changes which can support a healthy and balanced relationship with the water within our bodies and within the body of the earth. We can all play our part to deeply dive into nurturing hope for a more sustainable future for the Oceans, the Earth, and for all living beings. Awareness, creativity and ecological tips here in this book can inspire those who are exploring how to deepen with your heart centre in remembering the huge benefit that harmony and balance can bring to the alleviation of the stress's from ourselves, from the Oceans and from this blue jewel Earth, we all call home.

The Mermaid Stories

Writing these 3 creative short stories in the essence of the
Mermaid, Mer people, happened quite naturally.

They seemed to be the closest descriptive embodiment of the
watery beings who mythologically exist harmoniously with
the element of water and with the waters of the earth.

We are remembering too that we are mostly water.

Remembering the qualities of water- flow, renewal, emotion,
depth and soul. Mermaid/man/child can also be symbolic in
referring to exploring our own emotional depth, in to the
depths of consciousness, and connecting more with our own
innate intuition, accompanied with natural transformation.

Chapter 2

The Mermaid's Dream

We are one with the waters,

we are all one with all Seas and Oceans

The Mermaid's Dream

The light shimmers upon the water, which opens up the Ocean and in to the mermaid's dream. In the silver light reflects the waters of our Mother, connecting to the depths of her soul. A voice is calling, calling, calling, come home to the truth. Divine truth illuminating your heart's desires with a softness always known. Ancient memories are stirring within my soul. Dive in, join the other Mer- people, and remember your Mer -soul. Remembering the ancient dream. The Mermaids eternal dream taking her home to the Atlantean waters. Where upon the violet horizon, hues of light shining between spaces, sacred swan flies in from the heavens, caresses the sweet pregnant maiden who lives within these waters. Swimming deeply in to the depths of this ocean, where one meets the gentle dolphin who has been waiting patiently for all those who know the ancient wisdom of all waters and Oceans. Swirling energy emerges from the centre of the Ocean. The turquoise heart spinning dolphins come to the surface showing their faces within the Turquoise dolphin vortex. Sparkling joy at my homecoming, how my heart sings to be welcomed home by these Sirian Star beings. Dancing upon the crest of the wave, the violet flame water Angel comes in transmuting and clearing the way, now soothed, healed and transformed, she invites me to enter the turquoise water swimming through delicate, intricate, fragile sea coral, stardust light.

A pure crystalline palace to so many beings of light, one speaks to me to tell me I am entering the Lemurian Waters of Light. Shimmering azure crystal waters, beings living within the liquid light, Mermaids, Mermen, Mer-children, seahorses, turtles, dolphin, whales. These beings are keepers of ancient wisdom, harmonising the waters, bringing in more light. Silver iridescent waves, soothing Mother Earth's body, soothing Mother Earth's heart, remembering we are all her sons and daughters. In to the depths deeper than I have ever known, pockets of light give me oxygen, give me life.

The taste of salt upon my lips, diving deeper still a shimmering energy emitting vast quantities of light I see before me. There a crown of brilliance, a trident of peace, dear Neptune, King of the Ocean and his beloved Luara, Queen. A strand of Neptune's hair passes by me, I reach out, and grasp it gently.

I will always remember this moment of eternity. No words spoken, I blink to find the Waters of light are emitting an emerald light, shinning, deep below me a glow of radiance, brilliance, diving deeper in I go. Deeper in to the Ocean I find the Emerald fire alive and alight, tuning in to the theta, which awakens my ancient Mer- soul. As I pass the hidden emerald dragon. I swim and I feel like I have entered outer space, but I am still within the Ocean, I see Mother Earth as a radiant delicate light being, she speaks to me. I am the pearl, My luminescence is a light in the galaxy, that is needed. A pure light in this universe, in rhythm with the ancient essence of Mu. My shimmering body of water vibrates sensitively, just as your body does too, emitting the frequencies of pure love for you all.

We are one with the Waters, we are one with all Oceans and Seas. Water is the key to all life, water requires our love and care, it is time to change the way we are living, for the Oceans are the Earth's largest ecological system, the Oceans are under strain from our CO_2 emissions. Time now to live more lightly, with honour, love and respect for the waters within ourselves, each other, our rivers, our Seas, Our Oceans.

With the blessing of my Mer -Grandmother, I enter the portal through the illuminated waters. Here I am met by sacred golden dolphins, the protectors of the biosphere of Mother Earth's Oceans, they swim beside me and guide me to the eternal bridge of cosmic stars, grace and all divine flowing order.

This story was written from a series of verses that were

created with each painting that went on to become

The Mermaids Dream art exhibition

Exhibited by the Atlantic Ocean

in St Ives, Cornwall, UK

Chapter 3

The Mer-Children

All water is one,

one whole, one awareness.

The Mer-Children

Within the ancient town of Lyme Regis in Dorset, England, a place known where Mermaids, Mermen and Mer-Children have lived in a realm finer and more subtle than the Earthly realm. It was here that 3 young children, who both bare the signs of Mer-Children lived. They live a life of truth, which many have spent lifetimes trying to find. The Mer Children know wisdom deep within and they intend to share with all those who care about the future of humanity, of our Oceans and of our Earth.

They are here to relay to all who live on the land to truly think about the Seas and Oceans and how they affect you and me. So many in their busy lives can miss the concept of the connection humans have with the Seas and Oceans. The Oceans balance out this Planet, which pulls us in and pushes us out, knowing it holds the world's entire vibrations within its all-encompassing Ocean Shell. Listen now and redeem yourselves for this is the essence of a story that for the rest of time shall be on all shelves.

The Mer-Children Sapphire, Indigo and Emerald spend their days mingling as Humans with the town's folk, enjoying the blue skies whilst walking the land. No one has any idea they are from the Mer- realms, people are yet to hear them speak of their wisdom in relation to all seas and Oceans.

Upon a full moon lit night as I strolled along the beach the Mer- Children appeared emerging from the water, half human, half mermaid causing me to reflect within the realms of the deep. They choose to be the link, inviting all humans to remember that the Seas and Oceans of this beautiful Planet Earth are more blue than green. The Earth is covered by 71% of Water, our bodies too contain more or less the same ratio. We are more like the Ocean, than we are of the Earth, were the words I heard them whisper carried by the wind. The winds of change are blowing, they call me in to the Ocean, the Mer- Children guiding me and holding my hands. Their message to me began, the vibrations of pollution is affecting all of our waters, not just of the Oceans, but also of our Sons and Daughters, of the Humans and Mer- people.

Water is the source of all life, life some say began from the Sea creating you and me. All water is one, one whole, one awareness. Water is aware of all other water in the World and it is aware of you and me. It contains all vibrations that we all create, all love, all disharmony, a whole body of water vibrating frequencies.

Return to love, honour and respect of all Water within our bodies and within all Oceans and Seas. This return to love, to harmony helps all water, within ourselves, for it flows within the blood in our veins, all rivers flow to the Ocean of wholeness that is part of you and me. The Mer-children carry my Mer-soul diving deeper in to the waters, I caught the glimpse that they are my Daughters. Daughters of change, arrival on Earth, engage, igniting to save our Oceans and Earth, they have put out a request for the truth to be heard and they are keen to know how we can all together rise up and be heard. The Wise souls of the Mer Children swimming the Oceans of our consciousness deeper and deeper. Some kind of inner heart knowing encourages me to be a truth seeker. A seeker of the truth of the disharmony of our Waters, Seas and Oceans.

Immerse in to the depths of the Oceans, trusting always as the feeling of its supporting essence is always flowing. The Oceans require our immediate action, attention and loving intervention, for the future of the Oceans, for the future of the Earth, wake up please for we need your help. Humans please remember we are not separate, we are one of the same, each drop of water is part of the whole. We are all connected in oneness, as part of the delicate ecological system of our home this Earth. We call for a return for respect for ourselves, each other, our Oceans, our Earth if we are to evolve and grow.

The Mer-children take me even deeper in to the oceans of my own consciousness. It is urgent for change, any cause of Environmental damage or harm cannot be alone repaired with monetary value or material wealth. The subconscious of the Waters, Seas and Oceans will find it difficult to re balance itself if we continue with the huge volumes of our individual behaviours and activities, the individual and collective CO_2 emissions we are creating is being soaked up by our Waters, Oceans and Seas. The volume of CO_2 needs

urgently decreasing to give hope for our Oceans, we need to

steer away from the tipping point of Ocean Acidification with

intention for sustainable change and hope for the Waters of

our Earth to have space to recover. For the Oceans hold an

ancient key to all life within the Oceans and upon the Earth

from the smallest to the largest, we are all connected, from

the source of plankton, and the air that we breathe, we

receive between 50 to 85% of our oxygen from the Oceans,

via phytoplankton plants that live within the Oceans and

Seas. The Ocean is the largest ecological system on the Earth,

the essence of Water is the source of all life here on the Earth.

Our lifestyles are now prophesied for sacred sustainable

change, we are called to become Guardians of our Waters,

Seas and Oceans here upon this Earth, for the Mer-children

return to free us from illusions. They are revealing themselves to all those now, who truly sense the oneness that we all are

part of, the oneness of our beautiful Oceans, Our beautiful

home, our sparkling blue jewel Mother Earth.

This story was written during my expressive art module

during the MSC Napoli container shipwreck disaster at

Branscombe, Devon 18.01.2007

Chapter 4

The Grand Mer-Children

The element of flow, cleansing and feeling, assisting us

all back in to the remembrance of the love, for when

we love, we naturally protect.

The Grand Mer-Children

As the sun sets on the horizon of the sea along the coast in Devon, a place of mystery, where ancient woodlands meet the sea. The Mer Grandchildren gather together to sing their song. Holding hands as they immerse themselves in to the crystal clear sea water, their etheric mer energy awakens and they begin to remember their true nature, which at times can be forgotten. Within the element of water they can feel the static energies of the day cleansing from blending in with life on land during the day. The immersion in to the water lifts their spirits, where upon they sense their place within this vast sea, which is connected to the global Ocean, which mirrors the stars, the Cosmos. Floating, looking skywards, they all see Venus shining brightly in the sky. Sparkles of star shaped light dances upon the shimmering water that the children are in. They hold hands together and begin to sing a song as ancient as the beginning of our remembering of when life began in all its purity. A song without words, a song of fluid ancient melodies sung from their hearts whilst floating within the crystal starlit sea. So much joy is felt from their joining together within the ancient element of water, they promise one another they will return to the sea each evening for ever more. For they remember their fluidity, their flow, their true nature, which naturally supports them in remembering why they are here.

Here as guardians of the water, the rivers, the seas, the ocean, sharing their wisdom, and the messages from the mythical stories of the sea, the collective remembering that we are all made of the elements.

How we relate to the water within ourselves, the water we drink, the water within our rivers, seas and global ocean matters. Remembering water has memory and is imprinted with the energies that is around it, so choose wisely the environment you are in. Express love and gratitude to yourself, the water within, to the water you drink, the water you bathe in as well as to the rivers, seas and Oceans, all are connected to the global Ocean.

See past the lens of the modern aspects of living and remember your true nature the Grand mer children say.

Being in harmony with yourself, each other and with the elements, remember the water brings the essence of flow. Returning to the remembrance within, being still enough to feel the deeper truths of our very existence.

The Grand Mer children join with the Mer children and the Mermaid, Merman and the ancient threads that weave them together life time after lifetime, unified together as one within the element of water.

The element of flow, cleansing and feeling, assisting us all back in to the remembrance of the love that emits from our hearts, our true nature, which balances our very existence with this blue jewel planets heart centre.

Chapter 5

Ocean Stressors

Ocean Acidification

Ocean Warming

Ocean Deoxygenation

Ocean Stressors

Over the coming decades and centuries, ocean health will become increasingly stressed by at least these three interacting factors – Ocean seawater temperature rising, ocean acidification and ocean deoxygenation, causing substantial changes in marine physics, chemistry and biology. These changes will affect the ocean in ways that we are only beginning to understand. It is imperative that international decision-makers understand the enormous role the ocean plays in sustaining life on Earth, and the consequences of a high CO_2 world for the ocean and society.

Ocean Acidification

The ocean covers nearly three quarters of the Earth's surface, contains 96% of its living space, provides around half of the oxygen we breathe and is an increasing source of protein for a rapidly growing world population. However, human activity, such as burning fossil fuels is having an increased impact on this precious resource.

Ocean acidification is directly caused by the increase of carbon dioxide (CO_2) levels from the atmosphere rapidly being soaked up by the Ocean, which causes a reaction. When CO_2 enters the ocean it rapidly goes through a series of chemical reactions which increase the acidity of the surface seawater (lowering its pH). The ocean has already removed about 30% of anthropogenic CO_2 over the last 250 years, decreasing pH at a rate not seen for around 60 million years. This has slowed the accumulation of CO_2 in the atmosphere and the rate of global warming; without this ocean sink, atmospheric CO_2 levels would already be greater than 450 ppm.

However, the continuation of such a fundamental and rapid change to ocean chemistry is bad news for life in the sea; it will not only cause problems for many organisms with calcium carbonate skeletons or shells (such as oysters, mussels, corals and some planktonic species) but could also impact many other organisms, ecosystems and processes with potentially serious implications for society.

The average acidity of the upper ocean has already declined by around 0.1 pH unit (30% increase in acidity) since the industrial revolution and it is expected to further decline by about 0.3 pH units by the end of this century if CO_2 emissions continue at the current rate.

Ocean Deoxygenation

Ocean deoxygenation is the reduction of dissolved oxygen (O_2) in seawater. Climate change can influence oxygen levels in the ocean in several ways. This is certain to occur in a warmer ocean since higher temperatures reduce oxygen solubility. Warming is also likely to create a more stratified ocean, decreasing the downward oxygen supply from the surface.

Ocean acidification and nutrient run-off from streams and rivers can also contribute to deoxygenation. Fish and many other marine organisms depend on sufficient levels of oxygen to function, and may therefore be stressed by declining oxygen concentrations. Extended zones of low oxygen may result in the exclusion of such organisms. However, other organisms tolerant of low oxygen, particularly microbes are likely to flourish, altering the balance of communities.

ow oxygen levels in the ocean may also increase the amount of greenhouse gases in the atmosphere by changing feedback mechanisms involving methane and nitrous oxide. Current ocean models project declines of 1 to 7% in the global ocean oxygen inventory over the next century. However, there are considerable uncertainties regarding the scale and location of oxygen changes, and their ecological impacts.

Ocean Warming

Ocean warming over the last few decades is a result of the atmospheric temperature increase due to the 'greenhouse' effect. This warming is the outcome of the exchange of gases between the atmosphere and Ocean surface, their transfer and storage in the deeper waters. It is highly likely that Ocean warming will have effects on marine organisms and alter the distribution of species.

The immensity of the heat content of the Ocean with 90% of the energy warming of the earth system stored in the Oceans over recent decades. Already there has been a mean sea surface warming of 0.70 C over the last 100 years, and likely to increase by over 30 C in some ocean regions by the end of this century.

Over the coming decades and centuries, ocean health will become increasingly stressed by at least these three interacting factors - Rising seawater temperature, ocean acidification and ocean deoxygenation, causing substantial changes in marine physics, chemistry and biology. These changes will affect the ocean in ways that we are only beginning to understand. It is imperative that international decision-makers understand the enormous role the ocean plays in sustaining life on Earth, and the consequences of a high CO2 world for the ocean and society.

Some of the notes in this chapter are from the 'Oceans Under Stress' booklet - from Plymouth Marine laboratory, with permission to share this information. from Plymouth Marine Laboratory, UK.

To understand more of the whole picture of how crucial it is to respect and take care of the deeper reality of our watery body and waters of the Earth, we can then begin to make conscious changes for the future, changes which support a harmonious, healthier sustainable way forward for the health and future of Humanity, the Oceans and for the Earth as a whole. A more hopeful future is one where we reduce carbon dioxide emissions, transition to cleaner, renewable sources of energy and prevent the need for such large-scale adaptation. Making individual and collective commitment to respect and nurture the waters within our bodies, and with the waters of the Earth and with the Oceans. As once we acknowledge the deeper truth of the part we all play in the well being of our own personal health and the health of the Waters of the Earth. Then we can individually and collectively become guardians of our Oceans and alleviate some of the environmental stress from ourselves, from the global Ocean and from this beautiful Earth, we all call home.

Chapter 6

Plastics in the Ocean

"An illustration of the sheer magnitude of the problem is that as much as 51 trillion microplastic particles – 500 times more than stars in our galaxy – litter the seas."

UN News - Plastic is an epidemic, that needs changing.

Here are 10 Ways to

Rise Above Plastic

- Choose to reuse when it comes to shopping bags and bottled water. Cloth bags and metal or glass reusable bottles are available locally at great prices.

- Refuse single-serving packaging, excess packaging, straws and other "disposable" plastics. Carry reusable utensils in your purse, backpack or car to use at bbq's, or take-out restaurants.

- Reduce everyday plastics such as sandwich bags and juice cartons by replacing them with a reusable lunch bag/box that includes a thermos.

- Bring your to-go mug with you to the coffee shop, smoothie shop or restaurants that let you use them, which is a great way to reduce lids, plastic cups and/or plastic-lined cups.

- Go digital! No need for plastic CD'S DVDs and jewel cases when you can buy your music and videos online.

- Seek out alternatives to the plastic items that you rely on.

- Recycle. If you must use plastic, try to choose #1 (PETE) or #2 (HDPE), which are the most commonly recycled plastics. Avoid plastic bags and polystyrene foam as both typically have very low recycling rates.

- Volunteer at a beach clean up.

- Support plastic bag bans, polystyrene foam bans and bottle recycling bills.

- Spread the word. Talk to your family and friends about why it is important to reduce plastic in our lives and the nasty impacts of plastic pollution.

Notes above from Eco Watch site

Chapter 7

Ecological Friendly Tips

To Save the Planet

Information and ecological tips on ways to become

more ecologically responsible.

Ecological Friendly Tips

To Save the Planet

Created by "Save our Seas Foundation"

with permission from the executive of SOS - Dr Nadia

Brunyndonckx. Information and ecological tips on ways to

become more ecologically responsible.

Switch it off - Using electricity has a huge impact on the

planet: every time you switch on a light or surf the internet,

you create pollution.

Don't pollute and don't waste water -Clean water is

a very precious commodity. Think carefully about what you

put down the drain. Chemicals from cleaning products and

shampoos take years to break down affecting the balance of the marine environment. Don't take water for granted.

Take it home -Three times as much rubbish is dumped in the world's oceans as the weight of fish caught each year. Plastic items and cigarette butts top the list of rubbish cleaned from beaches.

Be greener -Use your purchasing power to make a difference. You can help influence greener manufacturers and retailers.

Recycle it - All over the world, tonnes of rubbish go to landfills or for incineration each year creating enormous pollution problems. By recycling and re-using, you can very quickly help to reduce this.

Get going- If there were fewer cars on the road, there would be less pollution. How often do you get a lift into town instead of catching the bus?

Start today- Now you know some simple tips to reduce your own impact on the planet. Taking responsibility for the future need not be a chore. Make sure to tell all your friends and family too.

Just remember, everything we do that pollutes the land will eventually pollute the sea and vice versa.

By starting today, you can make a difference for tomorrow.

For the full Eco-Friendly Tips to Save the Planet booklet-

see the free downloadable link below -

http://saveourseas.com/book/eco-friendly-tips-to-save-the-

planet/

In the effort to protect our oceans, the Save Our Seas

Foundation funds and supports research, conservation and

education projects worldwide, focusing primarily on

charismatic threatened wildlife and their habitats. Save Our

Seas, also stock some small book publications for younger

children.

Chapter 8

Poetry

Heart of the Ocean,

Heart of the Earth,

Heart of the People

Awaken new depths

Awakening to the call of the ocean

Within us all is the heart intelligence to remember

All water connects everything

Keep remembering the deeper truths

Everything is connected as one now and always

Now and always.

New ways of being in relationship with the water

Ever deepening into the remembering that

Water connects us all.

Depths to be explored within ourselves and within our

oceans.

Exploring, inquiry leading to feeling our way forward

Past is over, the present is here, and the future is to be co-created.

The coming together in the awareness of our oneness of the oceans and the earth.

Hearts within humans lead the way to protect our planet's heart.

Sustainable and loving the relationships emerge with the water within and with the global Ocean that protects this earth.

One Heart, One Global Ocean, One Blue Jewel Earth

Heart of the Ocean

Heart of the ocean, heart of the earth, heart of the people

What will it take to realise changing our relationship with

the ocean's is urgently called for.

The oceans are reaching in to our collective consciousness to

become aware of the changes we are all required to make as

Awakening Ocean Guardians.

Swimming in the shallows of our consciousness is complete,

here we have learnt much.

Awareness of the complex stresses within the global Ocean

warming, acidification, deoxygenation and sea levels rising.

The moment now is for awakening into the deepest waters of

our consciousness of the global Ocean of our earth

The all encompassing body of water that protects the

biosphere of our earth needs to remain well

Diving in deeper to the remembrance that when you love

deeply, you then naturally care and protect.

Feeling the love within your heart for the waters, the seas the

oceans can inspire heart centred sustainable ways forward

Love and reverence for the water within our bodies and

within our global Ocean as one.

One Heart, one global Ocean, one blue jewel Earth

All together as One, deeply interconnected with the ocean

co-creating a more caring and more natural chapter in the

book of existence with our beautiful Ocean and Mother

Earth.

Water

Water so clear

Essence of blue swirling, churning

The eternal bliss within and without.

Eternal in presence deeply known for all time.

So treasured

So precious

So Clear

So Your voice becomes clearer.

Speaking so clearly in a language all of your own

Your language unique so innocent and pure

I will listen to your voice forever, your divine wisdom

the essence of the Ocean forever...

Beautiful Water

Dance with me on the edge of the shore.

Silvery moonlight lighting us up in awe.

Amazement of life

Emotion of the water which replicates.

Flow with the feeling

that it's not too late.

Pay attention to its subtle vibrations,

for then we can open the gate

Gate to the deeper soul knowing of the water's wisdom.

Look closely within for it is already showing.

Sacred water

Water rushing, pouring

Opening of the mysteries within the heart

No more ignoring

Open the gate

Cleansing waters come forth.

Water, rushing, pouring

No more ignoring

Sacred Water, so pure, so clear.

Awaken intentions within our hearts so dear.

Cleanse our hearts

Cleanse our souls

Cleanse until we remember ancient wisdom of old.

Water, rushing, pouring

Opening of the mysteries within the heart

No more ignoring

Energy flowing

Energy washing

Energy clearing

Re awaken

Re awaken

Awake now

For the time for remembering

is here now.

Deeply diving in to Ocean

Waters

Caressing my soul for eons

Forever whispering memories back to me

Through my soul I feel your immense love dear Ocean.

All-encompassing love soothing my heart, soothing my soul.

My heart fills like a well overflowing with love

My heart like a delicate flower

Neither human or of matter

Divine delicate heart of tenderness

Heart of tender love.

Cosmic Tender light

Deeply diving in to the global Ocean Waters.

In the Light

In the light that we are all one

With the element of water

May we all move forward

With all-encompassing feelings

That can inspire us into a deeper relationship

With ourselves, each other and all water

Within our beautiful Blue Jewel Earth

World Oceans Day

8th June

World Oceans Day reminds every one of the major role the oceans have in everyday life. They are the lungs of our Planet and a critical part of the biosphere. Sometimes celebrated either side of the 8th if the 8th falls on a weekend. As time goes on its becoming Ocean week and month. The purpose of the Day is to inform the public of the impact of human actions on the ocean, develop a worldwide movement of citizens for the ocean, and mobilize and unite the world's population on a project for the sustainable management of the world's oceans.

Information from the UN World Oceans Day

https://unworldoceansday.org/

Notes and website links

The Essence of Water -Oceans Earth and Us website link –

Oceanessence.weebly.com – Zoe Hudson.

Ocean Acidification, Ocean de-oxygenation and Ocean

warming chapter – Some of these notes are from the Oceans

Under Stress booklet- with permission from Plymouth

Marine Laboratory, UK. - https://www.pml.ac.uk/

Plastics in the Ocean- Notes above from Eco Watch site.-

https://www.ecowatch.com/ocean-plastic-guide/

Ecological Friendly Tips To Save the Planet - Created by

"Save our Seas Foundation"with permission from the

executive of S.O.S - Dr Nadia Brunyndonckx-

https://saveourseas.com/

World Ocean Day Information from the UN World Ocean

Day https://unworldoceansday.org

About the Author

Zoe Hudson is an Environmental Artist, graduate of Plymouth University, poet and well being facilitator who in her exploration of the importance of well being with in the self, in relation to the water, the global Ocean, weaves together the creative essence of art, poetry, story and awareness together as a whole experience.

The Essence of Water Oceans Earth and Us, Art and Information Exhibition -Remembering Our Deeper Relationship with Water and Our Global Ocean- Experience through a collection of paintings, story, poetry and information discover more about the delicate nature of the Ocean and of how deeply we are all connected to the element of Water and the global Ocean, the largest ecological system on the Earth. With awareness we can all make conscious changes now and for the future, changes which can support

a more harmonious, healthier sustainable way forward for

the health and future of Humanity, the Oceans and for the

Earth as a whole. Zoe is also a friend of the United Nations

World Oceans Day and is on the Women 4 Oceans Map.